The
Chocolate Cake

Story by Dawn McMillan

Illustrations by Meredith Thomas

Sunday was a cold, wet day.
Tess and Nathan
looked out the window.
The rain bounced off the glass.

"It's still raining!" said Tess.
"It rained all day yesterday,
and we couldn't go camping."

"What are we going to do today?"
asked Nathan.
"We can't go outside.
The backyard is covered in water."

Tess thought hard.
"Let's ask Mom
if we can make a cake!"

"What a good idea," said Mom,
when they asked her.
"That will keep you busy!
You can make a chocolate cake.
There's a cake mix in the cupboard.
I'll turn the oven on for you."

"I've found the cake mix," said Tess.
"This will be easy to make," she said,
as she read the words on the box.
"We just need to use two eggs,
some butter, and a cup of water."

"Great!" said Nathan.
"Let's get started."

Nathan put the cake mix and the water
into the bowl.
Next, Tess broke the eggs carefully
and slipped them in.
Nathan held the bowl
and began to mix everything together.

"Wait until I put the butter in!"
said Tess.

The children took turns
at stirring the cake mixture
until it was thick and smooth.

"I think it's ready to cook,"
said Tess.

They poured it into a cake pan,
and then they put it into the oven.

"Let's lick the bowl," said Nathan.

Half an hour later,
the cake was done,
and Mom took it out of the oven.

Dad came into the kitchen.
"Yum!" he said.
"I can smell chocolate cake!"

Tess and Nathan were excited
about their cake.

"Wait until it's cool," said Mom.
"Then it will come out of the pan."

But the chocolate cake
did **not** come out of the pan.
It was stuck to the sides
and the bottom!

"I'll help you," said Mom.

"Too late!" cried Nathan.
"It's breaking!"

Part of the cake was on the plate,
and part of it was still stuck
to the pan.

"We made a mistake," cried Tess.
"We forgot to butter the sides
of the pan, first."

Nathan and Tess were upset.

"It's no good!" said Tess.
"It's all broken!"

Nathan looked at the broken cake.
"I've got an idea!" he said.
Then he whispered to Tess.

After dinner, Tess told Mom and Dad
to stay at the table.

Nathan put parts of the cake
into four bowls.

Tess cut up a banana
and put it on top of the cake.
"There's some custard in the fridge,"
she said to Nathan.
"Let's put that in the bowls, too."

She poured the yellow custard
into the bowls. It ran down
between the cake and banana.

"Now I'll put some ice cream on top," said Nathan.

"That looks wonderful!"
said Mom, when she saw
what Tess and Nathan had made.

"Mmmm!" said Dad. "It's delicious!
This is the **very** best kind
of chocolate cake!"